THE SATURDAY

A STORY FROM THE 1940s

Written by Patricia Cleveland-Peck
Illustrated by Jenny Press

Collins Educational
An imprint of HarperCollins*Publishers*

Chapter One

"He's here!" Annie's mum said. She came out of the kitchen drying her hands but Annie was already out of the front door, almost tripping over her dad's old motorbike. She had heard the clip-clop of Kipper's hooves even before Mr Allbright had turned the corner into their street.

Mr Allbright, who sold vegetables from his small cart, was always very welcome because this was the time of the Second World War. Most of the men were away fighting and women had to spend hours in queues waiting to buy what little food there was in the shops.

Annie waited eagerly at the gate, a small piece of apple damp and slippery in her hand. Mr Allbright came round every Saturday and seeing his pony, Kipper, was the time she looked forward to all week. Finally, they stopped in front of Annie and she felt Kipper's warm breath on her cheek and smelled his delicious pony smell. Carefully, she offered the apple with her hand quite flat and the pony picked the apple off it gently with his soft, whiskery mouth.

"Good lass," said Mr Allbright, climbing slowly down from the cart. "He knows you now, does our Kipper. He pulls up that hill smartish, looking for you."

Annie smiled, her face beaming with happiness. Mr Allbright, an old man with bristly white hair and pale blue eyes, grinned back at her.

While Mr Allbright weighed out the potatoes and sprouts for her mum, Annie stroked Kipper's head and combed his white mane. He was a lovely pale grey colour, dappled with deeper circles of grey on his little rounded rump. He was small, strong and very fit and twice as old as Annie. His eyes were dark and kind and his tiny ears, which moved backwards and forwards listening to all she said, were soft.

All too soon Annie heard Mr Allbright's familiar words as he climbed creakily back on his seat and picked up the reins,

"Well, best push on..."

Annie gave Kipper one last pat and whispered, "See you next week, my Saturday pony."

As it turned out, however, Annie did not have to wait a whole week.

One evening, her grandad came over with a salmon which he had caught from the river when no-one was looking. It was such a treat that her mum decided to cook them all a special meal.

"What I need to go with salmon," she said, "are some fresh new potatoes. I wonder if Mr Allbright's got any left over at the smallholding? We could walk over and see, Annie, it's not far."

Annie was overjoyed and ran most of the way there.

The smallholding was on the edge of the Downs. There were some little huts with chickens and three fierce-looking geese. There were beans and peas and lettuces growing in neat rows in the earth.

While her mum chatted to Mr Allbright, Annie found Kipper in his field. Without his harness he looked even more beautiful. When he saw Annie he whinnied and came trotting up to her at once.

"You know me!" she said happily as she hugged him and he snuffled her ear gently and blew into her curly black hair.

Mr Allbright and her mum came and watched them.

"You could let her come over again," Mr Allbright said. "She'd come to no harm here."

Annie's mum had known Mr and Mrs Allbright for years and so she agreed.

Chapter Two

Annie began visiting the smallholding after school. First of all she would say hello to Kipper and then she helped Mr Allbright water the young plants and feed the chickens and geese.

"You're a help, lass," he said to her. "A right good help. It's not so easy to get everything done now I'm getting on."

Sometimes Mr Allbright picked some fruit for Annie and she sat near Kipper while she ate it. With the sharp taste of redcurrants in her mouth, the sun on her back and Kipper nearby, she felt the most contented girl in the world.

Once Kipper accidentally trod on her foot. It was the worst pain Annie had ever known. It hurt so much that she couldn't even cry at first, only double up and gasp. Then she cried a lot. The next day there was a big, hoof-shaped bruise on her foot. But it didn't stop her loving Kipper.

One day, Mr Allbright was waiting for her with a smile on his face. He held up something old, made of leather.

"Look what I've found in the back of the stable," he said. "It's an old riding bridle. Do you want a go on Kipper's back?"

Annie nodded, speechless with delight.

"You can. He's been ridden before. My lad rode him when he was young."

First Annie learned how to clean the bridle with saddle soap and soften it with linseed oil. Then, with beating heart, she followed Mr Allbright slowly up the field.

Kipper stood quietly as Mr Allbright showed Annie how to put the bridle on. His hands were old and shaky but he managed it quite easily. Then he took it off and Annie tried. It was difficult at first, but she soon got used to slipping the bit into Kipper's mouth, pulling his ears gently through the straps and doing up the brass buckle.

Mr Allbright didn't have a saddle so when Annie climbed up onto Kipper's back she could feel his warmth through her old cotton trousers. It felt strange but she wasn't frightened. Mr Allbright led Kipper gently forward, explaining how to hold the reins so as not to pull Kipper's mouth. He told her lots of other things which she tried hard to remember and then, all too quickly, it was time to go home.

Soon Annie was riding all over the countryside. That summer she was so happy. Exploring the chalky tracks of the Downs on Kipper's back, the wind in her face and the skylarks singing overhead, she wished it could go on for ever.

"You're a natural, lass," Mr Allbright told her as he watched her trotting into the yard. "It's a real pleasure to see you on that little pony."

Because Mr Allbright still did his vegetable round on Saturday mornings, Annie was careful not to tire Kipper out on Fridays. Instead she groomed him extra well and helped Mr Allbright to pack the produce on the cart for delivery the next day.

And at home Annie still watched out for Kipper with a piece of apple for him.

Chapter Three

Then one awful Saturday Mr Allbright didn't come.

Annie waited all morning and then went up to the smallholding. Kipper was in his field and the cart was still exactly as they had left it but there was no sign of Mr Allbright.

Annie knew where he lived and ran all the way to his house. Out of breath, she knocked on the door. When Mrs Allbright opened it, Annie knew from her face that something terrible had happened. Mrs Allbright told Annie that her husband had died in the night.

Every day after that Annie went to the smallholding and looked after Kipper. She tried to do all the things which she had seen Mr Allbright do. She fed the chickens and collected the eggs. Then, with her legs shaking, she fed the horrid, hissing geese. She watered the young plants and harvested the vegetables. But the weeds grew very quickly and somehow she couldn't stop the smallholding becoming overgrown and neglected.

Every day she took the eggs and vegetables down to Mrs Allbright who called her a 'little angel'. However, they both knew this could not go on for ever.

"What are we going to do with Kipper?" asked Mrs Allbright. "I've got someone coming for the hens and geese but I don't know about the pony."

“Can *we* have Kipper?” asked Annie when she got home. Her dad was home on leave and he was busy cleaning his old motorbike. “Mrs Allbright said she doesn’t want Kipper going for cat’s meat. She said that would make poor Mr Allbright turn in his grave.”

"Where would we put him?" asked her dad. "The smallholding belongs to the council and I heard that they are going to build houses up there now the war is nearly over."

"Besides," said her mum. "What do we know about keeping ponies?"

Annie didn't reply. She knew everyone was busy planning what they would do when the war was over and that, to them, was far more important than what happened to her favourite pony.

The next time she went to see Kipper, Annie rode him out over the Downs and thought and thought. Who did know about keeping ponies? Then she had an idea. There was a big house on the main road with a pony in a field. Everyone said a mad woman lived there. A woman who hadn't spoken to anyone since her son had been killed in the battle of El Alamein. Annie shivered.

Still, she couldn't think of anything else she could do. So the next day she forced herself to set off.

As she walked up the long drive her heart thumped and she felt sick. When she saw the house, so big and old, she wanted to turn back.

Then she caught sight of the pony in his lovely big field. He was a dark bay, slightly bigger than Kipper and his tail swished lazily as he grazed. There were acres and acres of good grass, a copse of trees for shade and shelter and a clear stream for water. Annie thought of Kipper alone on the neglected smallholding and, although her legs felt wobbly, she continued to the front door.

"If she is really mad I can always run away," she said to herself. "I'm quite a good runner…"

But as soon as the door opened Annie saw that the woman was not mad at all, only sad. She had big dark eyes and her hair was white although her face was quite young.

Before setting off, Annie had gone over and over in her mind what she was going to say, but now that the time had come to say it her mind was blank.

"Are you collecting jumble for the Girl Guides?" the woman asked with a little smile. She had a soft, gentle voice. "You'd best come in."

Suddenly, Annie realised there was no reason to be afraid of this lonely woman. She followed her down a long passage into the kitchen. The woman, who said her name was Margaret Moyle, listened carefully when Annie explained that she hadn't come for jumble.

"My name is Annie Parker," she began and she told Mrs Moyle all about Mr Allbright and Kipper.

"Come and look," said Mrs Moyle when Annie had finished. Reaching for her coat she opened the back door and took Annie along a path which wound round some outbuildings and across the vegetable patch through a wicket gate. Mrs Moyle pointed to her son's pony in the field.

"His name is Tippet. He's a dear old boy. He belonged to my son, Brian," she said. "Brian thought the world of him. We used to have an old donkey too but since that went, poor Tip has been rather lonely. So your Kipper is welcome to come and keep him company. He can share the field. We've plenty of grass."

Annie held her breath. She hardly dared to hope.

"How much must I pay?" she asked.

"I don't know." Mrs Moyle shook her head. "A little grass, a little hay, it doesn't cost a great deal, so I wouldn't charge you much."

"I could help you in exchange," said Annie hopefully, looking at the vegetable garden. "Mr Allbright taught me to weed and look after plants. I could come for a couple of hours a week."

"That would be a very satisfactory arrangement," said Mrs Moyle, giving Annie an amused look. "You're a resourceful girl, Annie Parker, you deserve to get on. Now come inside and let me give you a piece of cake."

Over tea and cake beside the big old Aga in the kitchen, Annie remembered something else. Horseshoes were very expensive.

"Mum and Dad could never afford shoes for us every few weeks, let alone for a pony," she told Mrs Moyle, glumly.

Mrs Moyle explained that Kipper had only needed the shoes to go out on the road with the cart.

"In the field you can take his shoes off and it won't cost much for the blacksmith just to file his feet when he does Tippet's.

"It does mean you won't be able to ride him on the roads. But," she added, "you've got the Downs, which are much nicer, and there's a path all the way up from our woods."

Annie felt much happier, hearing this.

Then Mrs Moyle brought out a big box of photographs of her son, Brian, to show Annie.

There were pictures of him at school, pictures of him on the beach, pictures of him riding Tippet and, last of all, pictures of him as a soldier. Mrs Moyle said he had been killed fighting when he was only 19 years old.

"I hate the war," she said. "Thank goodness it's almost over. I hope you never have to go through anything like it again, Annie."

After they said goodbye, Annie skipped down the long drive. She looked back at the house. How silly she had been to be frightened. She felt very sorry about Mrs Moyle's son but nothing could stop her feeling happy about Kipper.

Chapter Four

Annie's mum was very surprised to hear that Annie had had the nerve to go and see Mrs Moyle. She was pleased about Kipper but was still a little concerned.

"What if he needs the vet? It could be expensive…"

"Look," said her dad. "We'll manage. It means a lot to our Annie, and I'm really proud of the way she's fixed it all up. I'll go down and see Mrs Allbright."

He returned an hour or so later with a glum face. He shook his head sadly.

"I'm sorry lass," he said. "Very sorry, but it's all off."

"Why?" asked Annie, panic rising inside her. "Mrs Allbright said if I could find somewhere for him I could have him."

"It's not her," replied her father. "She would still give him to you. It's the Allbrights' son. He wants money."

Annie knew how impossible this was. They just didn't have any money.

"You see he's got a new job up Wilford way," continued her dad, "And he needs transport to get there. You can't blame him really. He needs money and a pony is worth money. They can't afford to let him go for nothing."

Annie felt too upset to speak. It was so unfair. Mr Allbright's son didn't love Kipper, he only wanted money for him. And who would buy him? At the very best another child would get him and love him; that was hard enough for Annie to bear. At the worst he might end up, as so many old ponies did, at the slaughterhouse and that she could not bear at all.

Annie went to bed without saying another word and although she thought and thought, this time she knew there was nothing she could do. It was all so hopeless.

The next day at school she hardly spoke to anyone. Her teacher thought she must be sickening for something and kept asking her what was wrong. Annie just shook her head dumbly and waited for the end of the school day. Instead of going home, she went to the smallholding.

"I've come to say goodbye, Kipper," she whispered and putting her head against his neck, she cried softly.

When she got home, pale and tired, she found her mum and dad in a good mood. There was going to be a big street party to celebrate the end of the war and they were helping with the preparations. Annie was too upset to listen to her parents chatting about the party and how, in peacetime, everyone was going to have a better life. She heard the door shut and saw her dad leave on his motorbike. Where could he be going just before the party?

"Come here, love, you look terrible," said her mum, leaving her sandwich-making and lifting Annie onto her lap. Annie lay there like she had done when she was a baby and her mum hugged her.

"Just hang on a bit longer, love," she said rocking her to and fro. "Dad won't be long and then the party can start." Annie, exhausted, fell fast asleep.

As she slept, she missed hearing the sound of Kipper's hooves for the first time in her life, as he turned the corner into their street.

It wasn't until her dad stood outside, calling her name, that Annie woke up and scrambled off her mum's lap. She ran to the front door and opened it. There, in front of the house, under the bunting and flags, stood her dad, holding Kipper's halter.

"Take your pony, Annie," he cried with a nervous laugh. "Before he bites me!"

Amazed, Annie ran to Kipper and hugged him. She couldn't believe it. She turned to her parents who stood hand-in-hand looking at her.

"How?" was all she could ask.

"With his new job your dad is going to get a van from the firm," said her mum. "So I told him to go straight round and offer young Allbright his old motorbike. You know what a good one it is. Allbright needed a way of getting to work," she said with a smile. "Well, now he's got it!"

"Oh Dad," gasped Annie. "Is it all right?"

"Of course it is, love. A straight swap. He was pleased with the bike. I think he felt a bit mean about not letting you have the pony anyway. And you should have seen old Mrs Allbright's face. She was that delighted, and said now her old man would rest in peace. So, now he's yours. Come on."

And that is how Kipper, who started off as Annie's Saturday pony, ended up going almost everywhere with her, including the street party which celebrated the end of the war.